my itty-bitty bio

# Marie Curie

Published in the United States of America by Cherry Lake Publishing
Ann Arbor, Michigan
www.cherrylakepublishing.com

Content Adviser: Ryan Emery Hughes, Doctoral Student, School of Education, University of Michigan
Reading Adviser: Marla Conn MS, Ed., Literacy specialist, Read-Ability, Inc.
Book Design: Jennifer Wahl
Illustrator: Jeff Bane

Photo Credits: © Photos.com/Thinkstock Photos, 5; © Neveshkin Nikolay/Shutterstock, 7, 22; © Everett Historical/Shutterstock, 9; © Everett Historical/Shutterstock, 11; © Photos.com/Thinkstock Photos, 13; © Humdan/Shutterstock, 15; Photos.com/Thinkstock Photos, 17; © traveler1116/iStock Photo, 19, 23; © HUANG Zheng/Shutterstock, 21; Cover, 6, 12, 16, Jeff Bane; Various frames throughout, © Shutterstock Images



Library of Congress Cataloging-in-Publication Data

Names: Loh-Hagan, Virginia, author. | Bane, Jeff, 1957- illustrator.
Title: Marie Curie / by Virginia Loh-Hagan ; illustrator: Jeff Bane.
Other titles: My itty-bitty bio.
Description: Ann Arbor, Michigan : Cherry Lake Publishing, [2018] | Series: My itty-bitty bio | Includes index. | Audience: K to 3.
Identifiers: LCCN 2017029647| ISBN 9781534107151 (hardcover) | ISBN 9781534108141 (pbk.) | ISBN 9781534109131 (pdf) | ISBN 9781534120129 (hosted ebook)
Subjects: LCSH: Curie, Marie, 1867-1934--Juvenile literature. | Chemists--Poland--Biography--Juvenile literature. | Women chemists--Poland--Biography--Juvenile literature.
Classification: LCC QD22.C8 L64 2018 | DDC 540.92 [B] --dc23
LC record available at https://lccn.loc.gov/2017029647

Printed in the United States of America
Corporate Graphics

# table of contents



**About the author:** Dr. Virginia Loh-Hagan is an author, university professor, former classroom teacher, and curriculum designer. Like Marie, she worked her way through school. She lives in San Diego with her very tall husband and very naughty dogs. To learn more about her, visit: www.virginialoh.com.

**About the illustrator:** Jeff Bane and his two business partners own a studio along the American River in Folsom, California, home of the 1849 Gold Rush. When Jeff's not sketching or illustrating for clients, he's either swimming or kayaking in the river to relax.

my story

I was born in Poland. It was 1867.

Only men went to school. It wasn't fair. I took secret classes.

I moved to Paris. I studied **science**.

What do you want to study?

I worked at night. I was poor.

I was hungry. But I didn't give up.

I met Pierre Curie. He loved science, too.

We married. We set up a **lab**.

Do you like working in teams?

I was a woman.
People doubted me.

I worked harder.

I tested **rays**. I found new **elements**. My work made sick people better.

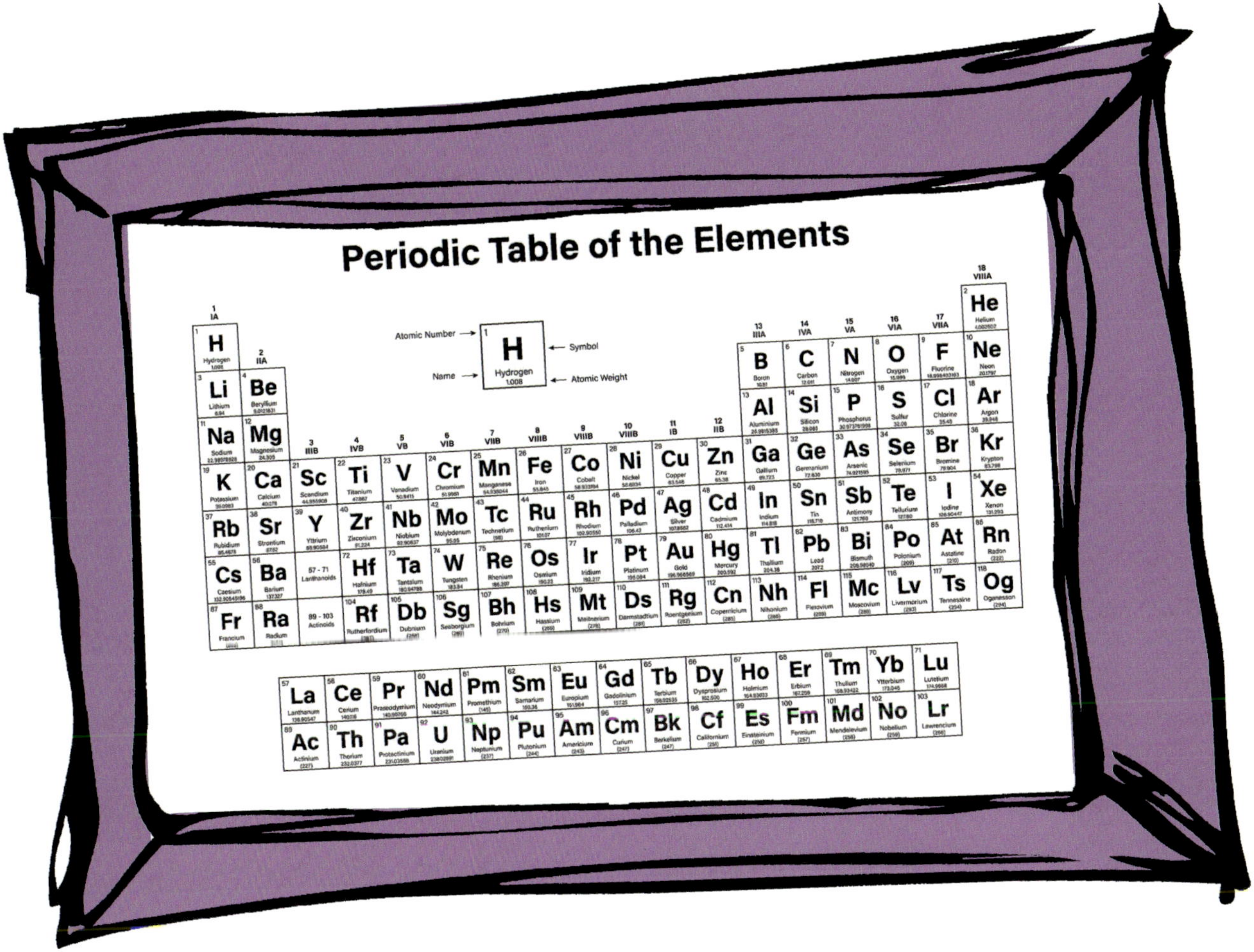
Periodic Table of the Elements
Atomic Number
Symbol
Name
Atomic Weight
H
Hydrogen
1.008
H He
Li Be B C N O F Ne
Na Mg Al Si P S Cl Ar
K Ca Sc Ti V Cr Mn Fe Co Ni Cu Zn Ga Ge As Se Br Kr
Rb Sr Y Zr Nb Mo Tc Ru Rh Pd Ag Cd In Sn Sb Te I Xe
Cs Ba Hf Ta W Re Os Ir Pt Au Hg Tl Pb Bi Po At Rn
Fr Ra Rf Db Sg Bh Hs Mt Ds Rg Cn Nh Fl Mc Lv Ts Og
La Ce Pr Nd Pm Sm Eu Gd Tb Dy Ho Er Tm Yb Lu
Ac Th Pa U Np Pu Am Cm Bk Cf Es Fm Md No Lr

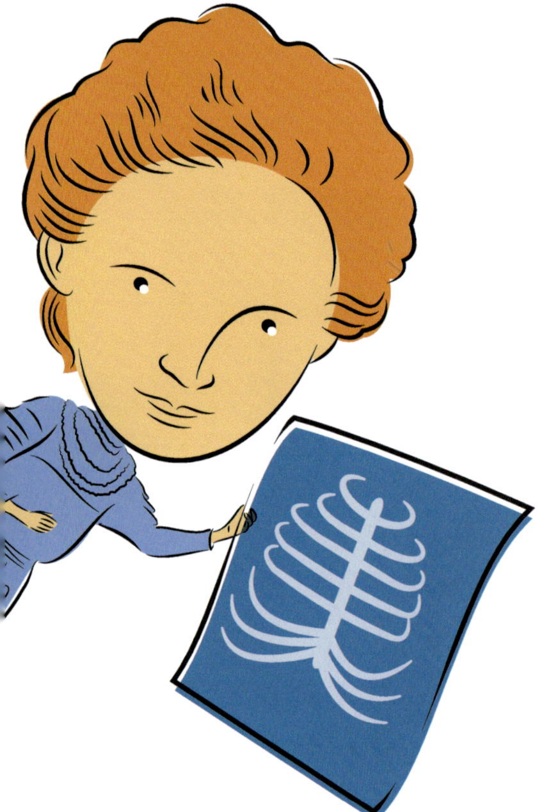

There was a war. Soldiers died. Doctors needed help.

I made special trucks. The trucks carried **x-ray** machines.

What helpful ideas do you have?

I won two Nobel Prizes. These go to people who do important work.

I was the first woman to win.

NOBELPRIS 1903
BECQUEREL
P CURIE
M CURIE
SVERIGE 50

I got sick. I died in 1934. I loved learning.

I **inspire** others. I showed women can be **scientists**!

What would you like to ask me?

timeline

1891

1860

Born
1867

1903

1960

Died
1934

glossary & index

## glossary

**elements** (EL-uh-muhnts) things that have weight and take up space and cannot be broken down

**inspire** (in-SPYRE) to fill someone with a feeling or an idea

**lab** (LAB) a place to do science projects

**rays** (RAYZ) energy that comes off things

**science** (SYE-uhns) the study of nature and the world we live in

**scientists** (SYE-uhn-tists) people who study science

**x-ray** (EKS-ray) a way to see inside the body to find out problems

## index